SUPER CITIES!

NASHVILLE

by Mark Shulman

arcadia
CHILDREN'S BOOKS

Published by Arcadia Children's Books
A Division of Arcadia Publishing
Charleston, SC
www.arcadiapublishing.com

Copyright © 2022 by Arcadia Children's Books
All rights reserved

Super Cities is a trademark of Arcadia Publishing, Inc.

First published 2022

Manufactured in the United States of America.

ISBN 978-1-4671-9889-9

Library of Congress Control Number: 2022937946

Produced by Shoreline Publishing Group LLC
Santa Barbara, California
Designer: Patty Kelley

Contents

WELCOME TO Nashville!

When you say "Nashville," most people think of three things: music, music, and, oh yeah, country music. That's true, but even in a place nicknamed Music City, USA, there's a whole lot more.

Nashville is a lovable, livable mid-sized city with great people, great neighborhoods, great food, great sports, and great things to do. Along with the nonstop music, you'll find a busy arts scene, beautiful scenery and parks, festivals, and plenty for kids to do. Just walk along busy Broadway and you'll experience the sights, sounds, and sizzle of this city.

There's also rich American history in Nashville. It's the capital of Tennessee—America's 16th state—which joined the Union under

FAST FACTS

Nashville, Tennessee

POPULATION:
692,000

FOUNDED:
1779

NICKNAME:
Music City, USA; Athens
of the South

President George Washington! From the elegant capitol building to beautiful old neighborhoods, Nashville is a time traveler's delight!

But back to the music for a moment. Here is where bluegrass and country music are always happening. It begins on street corners and small stages . . . grows in recording studios and concert halls . . . and ultimately gets honored in the Country Music Hall of Fame! This genuine American art form knows no bigger home than Nashville.

It's easy to go on and on about Nashville's cultural riches and natural beauty , but that's what this book is for. Let's go!

Nashville is the largest city in the state of Tennessee, in both size and population. The city is in the middle of the state, with the Cumberland River flowing through it. The main part of downtown is south of the river. To the east, a small dam called the Old Hickory Lock blocks some of the flow of the river, forming a wider part, almost like a long, thin lake. A larger body of water, the Priest Reservoir, is to the southeast of the city. Forests and rolling hills form the western border of the Nashville area.

After beginning as a settlement in the 1700s, the city grew over many years, thanks to agriculture, especially cotton, as well as iron mining, railroads, and shipping. So many people moved in that by the 1950s, the city had added more than 40 square miles to its borders.

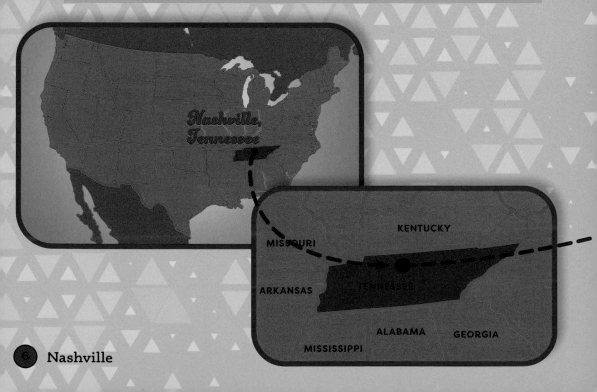

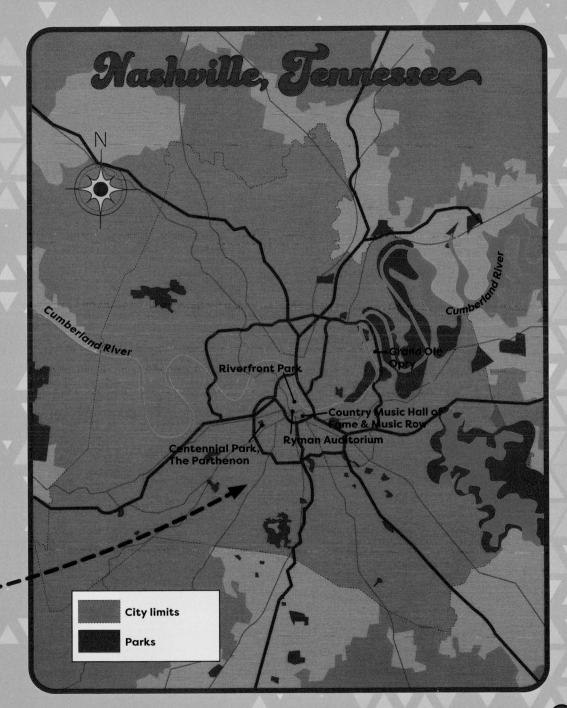

Nashville, Tennessee

N

Cumberland River

Cumberland River

Riverfront Park

Grand Ole Opry

Country Music Hall of Fame & Music Row

Ryman Auditorium

Centennial Park, The Parthenon

City limits

Parks

Music City, USA

Why is Nashville called *Music City, USA*? From its nearly 200 music venues to its many recording studios, TV shows, and museums, no other city has such deep roots in country, bluegrass, gospel, blues, rock, and pop music. In Nashville, live music is everywhere, every day.

Because of its river and railroads, Nashville has always been a hub for travelers. Musicians are often on the move, and many early folk and blues musicians who found their way to Nashville stayed. Importantly, many enslaved Africans brought to Nashville also carried their music with them. These African influences are a vital part of the roots of American music.

Nashville's also called the *Songwriting Capital of the World*. Countless musicians come here to create, produce, and publish their music. Many of the most famous call Nashville home.

The best-known place for hearing Country Music is at the historic **Grand Ole Opry**.

Davy Crockett, one of Nashville's most famous historical figures, was a well-known fiddle player!

The famed **Music Mile** is a downtown stretch that encompasses every aspect of music, from the elegant Symphony Center complex, past the music businesses on Music Row, leading to the Country Music Hall of Fame.

NASHVILLE MEANS...

If you think Nashville was named for some guy named Nash, you're absolutely right! Brigadier General Francis Nash was a Revolutionary War hero.

Was he born near Nashville? Nope, Virginia.

Did he die there? Nope, Pennsylvania.

Well, his army regiment was from Tennessee, right? No indeed, it was from North Carolina.

But a new US Army fort was built in 1779, and Nash died a hero in 1779. So they named the place Fort Nashborough. Guess where it was? Five years later, the village around the fort changed its name to Nashville.

As for the state Nashville is in, Tennessee was named for the region's indigenous people, the Tanasi.

FRANCIS NASH

Patriot general in American Revolution, was mortally wounded at Germantown, 1777. His home is 150 yds. W.

FAST FACT

The *ville* in Nashville is the French word for *town*.

A replica of Fort Nashborough is in downtown Nashville. You have to go to Pennsylvania to see Nash's grave (bottom left).

FAST FACT

The *borough* in Nashborough comes from the Old English word burg, a fortified settlement.

THE GRAND OLE OPRY!

In 1925, in the earliest days of radio, station WSM's *Barn Dance* was broadcast from a Nashville insurance building called the Ryman Auditorium. It featured a parade of country singers and musicians. As the radio show grew—and performances were broadcast—it was renamed *The Grand Ole Opry* in 1927 ("opry" being a country version of the word "opera"). And the audiences grew, too. The Opry outgrew the Ryman, and in 1974 moved to its new home, which seats 4,000 fans.

Today the Opry's many concerts make up the world's longest-running radio broadcast of any kind. Its stages have featured thousands of talented country musicians, from long-ago singing cowboy Roy Rogers to a teenage Elvis Presley to today's stars like Darius Rucker and Keith Urban. Players played, records were made, and careers were launched— all under the Opry's historical roof.

> **FAST FACT**
>
> Opryland USA (1974-1997) was a now-closed country music theme park built around the Opry itself.

The adjacent Opryland Hotel is still among the world's largest, with 2,888 rooms. Go big or go home, right?

Find out about the roots of bluegrass at the Grand Ole Opry, too. A statue of bluegrass legend Bill Monroe is outside.

HISTORY: Early Days

People have been living in central Tennessee for perhaps 10,000 years. Scientists have found evidence of different Indigenous peoples' camps while doing archaeological digs. Many of these peoples' descendants still live in the area.

Clovis period: The first people to arrive in North America are sometimes called the Clovis, after a site in New Mexico where some of the first evidence of their existence was found. Arrowheads used by Clovis people have been found in Tennessee.

Mississippian: This widespread culture appeared about 1,000 years ago. Along with farming, the Mississippians used pottery and created types of artwork for ceremonies. Some scientists connect these people directly to the Indigenous tribes of Tennessee.

Woodland: About 3,000 years ago, people developed ways to grow their own food, instead of just hunting and gathering. This practice was called cultivation. Early people in Tennessee ate a lot of fish and shellfish from the rivers. Mounds of empty shells have been dug up near Nashville-area rivers, evidence of ancient landfills. These "woodland" people also created large burial mounds, which can still be seen in the landscape.

You can visit the site of a Mississippian village in Nashville. A park called Aaittafama' is on Old Hickory Boulevard. It has been restored with educational signs to help you explore this long-ago culture.

Before European settlers arrived in the area that became Nashville, several groups of Indigenous people made regular hunting trips to central Tennessee, though it appears few had permanent settlements here. Some were established tribes. Others were from groups that had been driven out by Spanish explorers to the south and west. By the 1700s, the largest local tribes were the Shawnee, Tanasi, Cherokee (left), and Chickasaw.

1500s–1600s: The Spanish explorer Hernan de Soto explored the Nashville area. French fur traders followed soon after, attracted to the animals living along the Cumberland River.

Cherokee: They controlled large amounts of land in what is now eastern Tennessee. The Cherokee hunted into the central part of the state near Nashville, and had hunting lodges and camps there. The US government forcibly took over most of the Cherokee people's land in 1819, leaving them a small portion in Tennessee. A National Forest is named for the Cherokee where some of that land was, at the North Carolina border.

Chickasaw: They hunted in western Tennessee, but by 1818 had been forced by the US government to give up most of their land.

HISTORY: Nashville Begins

1689: Martin Chartier set up a trading post near the salty land that was soon called "French Lick." Animals came to the area for the salt, and were then hunted. Their fur and meat were traded with the native people.

1779: During the Revolutionary War, Fort Nashborough (right and background) was built in the Tennessee wilderness to defend the land against the British Army. Apparently, it worked, as the British never took over Tennessee.

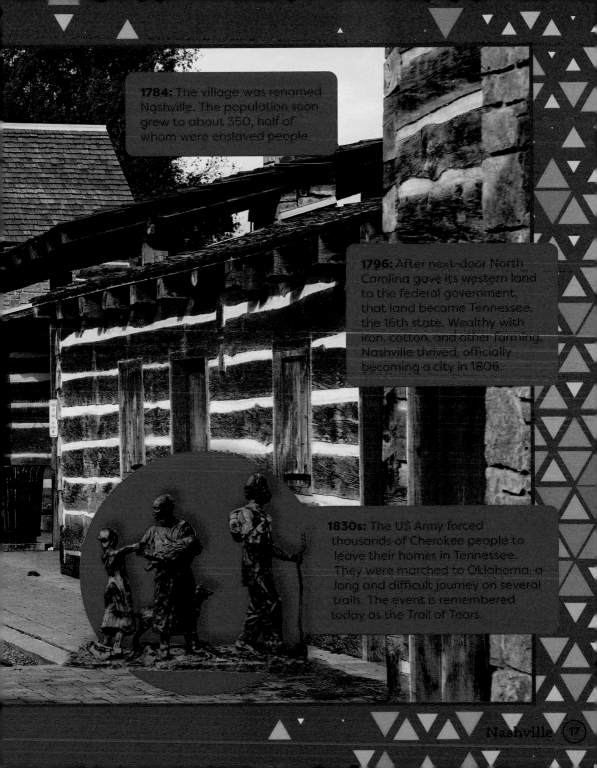

1784: The village was renamed Nashville. The population soon grew to about 350, half of whom were enslaved people.

1796: After next-door North Carolina gave its western land to the federal government, that land became Tennessee, the 16th state. Wealthy with iron, cotton, and other farming, Nashville thrived, officially becoming a city in 1806.

1830s: The US Army forced thousands of Cherokee people to leave their homes in Tennessee. They were marched to Oklahoma, a long and difficult journey on several trails. The event is remembered today as the Trail of Tears.

HISTORY: It's A City!

1843: A number of Tennessee towns competed to be Tennessee's permanent capital. In 1843, Nashville won by a single vote. Every vote counts!

1849: A deadly cholera epidemic killed 627 people, including ex-President James K. Polk. Another outbreak killed 1,000 people in 1873.

FAST FACT

During the War of 1812, Tennessee native (and future president) Andrew Jackson rose to fame, fighting the British alongside the Tennessee militia in the Battle of New Orleans.

1859: The Tennessee State Capitol building was completed, built by paid workers, prisoners, and enslaved people. It was both impressive and expensive, and it made a big show of Tennessee's wealth.

1861-1862: On June 24, soon after Abraham Lincoln's election, Tennessee became the 15th and final state to secede from the Union and join the Confederacy in the Civil War. Eight months later, in February 1862, Nashville was the first Confederate capital to be captured by Union forces.

1864: The Confederacy, eager to regain the city, attacked the Union on December 15 during the Battle of Nashville (background). They lost. Nashville (and the rest of Tennessee) was readmitted to the United States in 1866. Union soldiers stayed until 1877.

1897: The world came to Nashville for that year's World's Fair in what is now Centennial Park. It was a huge success. Of several dozen huge plaster buildings, the centerpiece was a copy of the Parthenon temple from Greece. It was so popular, the crumbling temporary building was fixed up and made permanent in 1925.

HISTORY: Nashville Grows Up

1900s: In modern times, the Nashville skyline began a-changing. Courthouses, office buildings, and grand music halls sprung up, bringing another side of Nashville's wealth back home to its residents.

1916: Disaster! The Great Fire of 1916, carried by strong winds, destroyed more than 500 buildings in East Nashville. Miraculously, only one person died, and very few were injured.

1920: The 19th Amendment of the Constitution was passed, giving American women the right to vote. The all-male Tennessee legislature cast the vote that made it official.

1925: The Grand Ole Opry arrived on radio station WSM, bringing Nashville's country music to listeners across the country.

 Nashville

The AT&T building (far left), Nashville's tallest at 617 feet, is often called the *Batman building*. Can you guess why?

1960s: Civil rights sit-ins and protests for equal rights for Black people led to Nashville's integrated future. See more on page 22.

1961: The Country Music Hall of Fame opened in 1961.

1969: Minnesota's most famous folk singer, Bob Dylan (left), came to record his country album, *Nashville Skyline*, with Johnny Cash (right) and other country musicians. The album's popularity is credited with bringing new life to Nashville's country music industry.

2000s: With its skyscrapers, mass transit, downtown entertainment complex, and pro sports teams, today's Nashville has become a true 21st-century city.

Nashville and Civil Rights

In the 1950s and 1960s, many students from Nashville HBCUs (see box) participated in Civil Rights protests. At that time, Black people weren't allowed to do many things that white people could, including sit in most Nashville restaurants. In 1960, at the lunch counter of Woolworth's department store, John Lewis (right, later a US Congressman) and more than 200 college students staged peaceful sit-ins. They were arrested for refusing to give up their seats. Due to these protests, Nashville became the first segregated Southern city to begin changing their unfair laws. That location is now a Civil Rights monument called Woolworth on Fifth. More exhibits about Nashville's Civil Rights history are on display at the Nashville Public Library.

FAST FACT

At the National Museum of African American Music, the contributions of Black musicians to blues, jazz, folk, bluegrass, and country music are celebrated with exhibits, music, videos, and more.

JOHN LEWIS, 1941

John Lewis

HBCU CITY Nashville's Historically Black Colleges and Universities (HBCUs) are among the nation's best schools. Fisk University (founded 1865) is Nashville's oldest existing college. Its Fisk Jubilee Singers (below in 1875) are world famous. The American Baptist College, Meharry Medical College, Tennessee State University, and Walden University are also in Nashville. Notable alumni include Ida B. Wells and W.E.B. Du Bois, as well as entertainer Oprah Winfrey, poet Nikki Giovanni, and many more.

Ida B. Wells

W.E.B. Du Bois

Oprah Winfrey

People from the Past!

Take a look at some of the people who have helped shape Nashville's history.

Moses (1879–1952) and Calvin (1890–1968) McKissack

In 1922, the McKissack brothers teamed up to create the first Black-owned architecture firm in the country. They built important buildings in Nashville, Washington DC, and other major cities. The company remains active today, led by Deryl McKissack, the fifth generation in the family. The firm designed the National Museum of African American History and Culture in Washington DC (right).

Hank Williams (1923–1953)

The first country music superstar, Hiram "Hank" Williams has inspired generations of musicians. He was also a gifted songwriter. While living in Nashville, Williams wrote an incredible 12 number-one country-and-western singles, and 55 that went to the top ten. Sadly, Williams lost his battle with addiction, and he died at the age of 29.

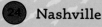

Wilma Rudolph (1940–1994)

Rudolph overcame childhood scarlet fever and polio—she was in a leg brace until age 11—to become one of the greatest female track-and-field athletes ever. She won three gold medals at the 1960 Olympics, the first woman ever to do so. At her insistence, the welcome home parade (to Clarksville, northwest of Nashville) was the first integrated event in the city's history. She was later a teacher and a coach.

Diane Nash (b. 1938)

While attending Fisk University in Nashville, Nash, a Chicago native, saw what life was like in the South for Black people. She began to work to change it, taking part in sit-ins and boycotts. She helped form the Student Nonviolent Coordinating Committee, as well as took a risk to become a Freedom Rider. In 2022, President Biden awarded Nash the Medal of Freedom for her Civil Rights work.

Nashville is the 21st largest city in the USA. Here's why its residents think it's Number One!

Friendly Folks: You've heard of Southern hospitality? People will go out of their way to help you or give you great suggestions. Forget the name: Nashvillians are the farthest thing from villains!

Amazing Eats: Hot chicken, sweet tea, and barbecue are the most famous choices. But Nashville has an endless supply of world-class restaurants of every cuisine.

It's Historic: Nashville's history is America's history. From the Revolution to the Civil War to Civil Rights, Nashville has always been in the middle of it all. You'll find buildings and treasures representing each era.

Beautiful Nature: Whether you prefer drives and hikes along the river, the rolling hills, the summer greenery, the autumn colors, or something else, you'll definitely prefer the city's moderate temperatures all year long.

Every Kind of Art: Do you love all kinds of museums? Architecture? Public art? Live music of every kind? Nashville offers great activities . . . every day!

Nashville Weather

If you want to experience four seasons, but not *too much* of any of them, you'll love Nashville.

Like most places in the South, the best times to visit are in fall and winter, when the temperature ranges from 50-70 degrees.

It's (almost) always sunny in Nashville, with 208 days of sunscreen needed a year. It rains (sometimes) or snows another 117 days each year, and the remaining 40 days each year are just plain cloudy! There's almost never more than 10 inches of snow each year.

Nashville does get hot in the summer, when the high temperatures can average 90 degrees in July and August. On the flip side, December and January aren't so cold, with low temperatures just below freezing, at 28 degrees.

The Tennessee Tornadoes

If you're a weathervane in Nashville, you get quite a workout. Nashville is in what's called Dixie Alley, a part of the south that gets several tornadoes a season. Central Tennessee averages 17 tornadoes per year. Hang on tight! On March 2, 2020, the deadly EF-3 and EF-4 tornadoes that hit the Nashville area were among the costliest in US history.

FAST FACT

Why are Christmas lights always shining bright on the historic RCA Studio B music building? In the 1950s, while recording a Christmas album in the summertime, superstar Elvis Presley needed help getting into the spirit. So the lights went up, and they haven't come down since!

Things to see in Nashville

Music Row is a name given to the part of downtown where lots of musical history was made—and is still being made today. It's a series of recording studios and publishing houses and theaters, packed with the artists and professionals who make up the heartbeat of country music.

One of the most famous recording studios is **RCA Studio B**. Built in 1956 by the RCA Victor record company, thousands of artists have made their music here. In this studio in the early 1960s, country star Chet Atkins helped create a new "Nashville Sound" which revived that style of music and brought even more artists to the studio.

Each of the nearly 100 stars on the **Music City Walk of Fame** features a tribute to a music industry artist or other professional. Find the trail on Demonbreun Street, nestled between the arena, the symphony center, and the Country Music Hall of Fame & Museum.

The Parthenon

The place was Centennial Park. The year was 1897, when world travel was difficult and Nashville hosted the World's Fair. To help people feel they had traveled far and wide, a variety of international buildings were built. They were made of plaster, designed to last just a few years. But one building was different—an exact-size duplicate of the famous Parthenon temple in Athens, Greece. Long after the fair ended, Nashville kept its beloved Parthenon, rebuilding the temporary, patched-over plaster building with permanent materials in 1925 .

Inside Nashville's Parthenon sits a 42-foot statue of the Greek goddess **Athena**, erected in 1990. That's fitting, since the original Parthenon was her temple— and the original Parthenon in Greece has a statue of Athena, too, except it dates back to 438 BCE.

FAST FACT

The whole building is about the size of half a football field.

The Parthenon may be a copy, but the art museum behind the pillars is an original. The **Cowan Collection of American Art** features landscapes, portraits, and temporary exhibits.

More Things to See

Historic Homes Tell Stories

To study Nashville's storied history, take a close look at a few homes with stories to tell.

Ten miles from Nashville is **The Hermitage**, President Andrew Jackson's 1804 cotton plantation. It hasn't changed much since 1845, the year Jackson died. It's a museum that explores the lives of Jackson and the farm's enslaved people, and it's the best-preserved early American presidential home. During a tour, experience stories of slavery through the eyes of the 100 or more people Jackson owned.

On another historic plantation, the **Belmont Mansion** is beautifully restored and maintained, preserving both its good and bad history. The original grounds had its own zoo. It has since been used as an education center and, most recently, as a museum.

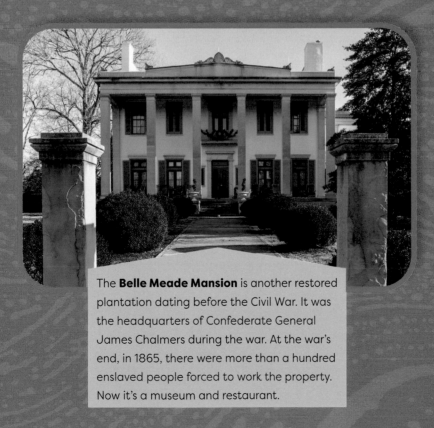

The **Belle Meade Mansion** is another restored plantation dating before the Civil War. It was the headquarters of Confederate General James Chalmers during the war. At the war's end, in 1865, there were more than a hundred enslaved people forced to work the property. Now it's a museum and restaurant.

GETTING AROUND
NASHVILLE

Nashville is the nation's 21st biggest city. Since it's so big, you can't always walk to get where you need to go. Check out WeGo, it's the modern mass transit system that will get you from point A to point B.

Buses: There are about 250 WeGo buses running along 54 different routes throughout the region. Two dollars will take you anywhere until 11pm. Also, Music City Circuit bus routes hit the main attractions downtown. And they do it for free!

Commuter Trains: The WeGo Star trains will take you 32 miles east of town, all the way to Lebanon, Tenn.

B-Cycle: These bikeshare bikes are found almost everywhere around town, so you can ride almost anywhere (and get some exercise, too!).

Golf Carts? Yes, golf carts! They take weary walkers around the downtown area for no charge. Tipping is encouraged.

Cities and states choose a lot of different things to make "official" for their places. Here is some of the official stuff for Nashville.

THE OFFICIAL SEAL AND FLAG OF NASHVILLE:

The city's official seal shows a Native American holding a skull. Uh, what's the deal there? In 1949, Mayor Thomas Cummings investigated just why that is and found that the person is supposed to be Chief Oconostota of the Cherokee. Supposedly, the skull (and other things around him) were going to be buried as a symbol to the end of the war between the Cherokee and the American army. Since it wasn't really a war as much as an unfair takeover of the Indigenous people by the colonists, it's an odd symbol.

OFFICIAL AMPHIBIAN:
Ever wonder what this little creature might be? Wait no more. It's the **Tennessee Cave Salamander**, a favorite found in the region's limestone caves.

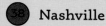

OFFICIAL BIRD:
In 1933, the **mockingbird** became the official state bird of Tennessee. Like many musicians, it's great at carrying many different tunes.

OFFICIAL MINERAL:
Agate, a colorful variety of quartz, was promoted from state rock (1969) to state mineral (2009).

OFFICIAL FLOWER:
There are many colors of iris, but the **purple iris** is Nashville's official flower.

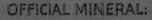

Art in Nashville

You won't believe how much art can be found on the streets of Nashville—nowhere near a museum.

History Art: This mural in Nashville shows the horsey way that people used to get around the city more than 150 years ago.

Riverside Art: One of Nashville's most famous outdoor sculptures is officially called *Ghost Ballet for the East Bank Machineworks*. It may look like a broken roller coaster, but it's got a great riverside location.

Museums Go See 'Em!

The Frist Art Museum is a downtown jewel. Since 2001, the Frist has featured a wide range of local and international art and artists. There's always something new to see, because the Frist doesn't have its own collection. It constantly creates and brings in new shows.

Martin ArtQuest is the Frist's interactive art area. Kids and adults can try their hands at printmaking, animation, painting, and shadow theater, plus explore amazing creative toys that aren't so easy to describe.

FAST FACT
In its first life, the Frist building was an historic 1930s post office.

The National Museum of African American Music: Just opened in 2021, the NMAAM is the only museum dedicated to the more than 50 music genres and styles that were created, influenced, and/or inspired by African Americans, including spirituals, blues, jazz, gospel, R&B, and hip hop. The six galleries feature everything music-related, from physical items to media and interactive technology.

The **Tennessee State Museum** is one of the best state museums anywhere. This huge museum displays the state's history, achievements, and notable people. The Tennessee Time Tunnel gives an overview of how Tennessee has grown. Interactive and hands-on displays are featured, as well as art, photos, crafts, historic, and military items. There's also an old print shop, along with fun ways to make your own creations.

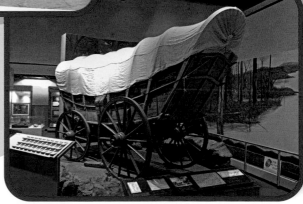

More Museums

If you like cars, including weird ones you've never seen before, then you'll love the **Lane Motor Museum**. There are more than 500 memorable vehicles: one-of-a-kinds, foreign cars, motorcycles, and bicycles going way back. Some of the cars fly (yes, fly) and others can float.

Adventure Science Center: From beekeeping to plasma to nanotechnology to rainforests, there is definitely going to be something for everyone to geek out about at this great place. Packed with hands-on activities, places to play and explore, and even cool VR and motion simulator rides, the Adventure Science Center is a day (or more!) of fun.

Gallery of Iconic Guitars:
Located at Belmont University, the GIG (get it? A gig is a musical event!) includes more than 500 stringed instruments from the collection of Steven Kern Shaw. He left them to the school, which has added many more classic guitars, mandolins, banjos, and other instruments. Imagine what it would sound like if they were all played at once!

Cheekwood Museum of Art (and Botanical Garden!): Coffee built this awesome mix of an art museum, a historic house, and a beautiful garden. The Cheek family made a fortune in groceries, but also created Maxwell House Coffee. It was one of the biggest brands in the United States for years. The house they built in Nashville has become this multi-use site, with lots of history and beauty to explore.

Nashville 45

Performing Arts

Nashville's Ryman Auditorium is called "The Mother Church of Country Music." And it's had many lives. In 1892, it opened as the Union Gospel Tabernacle, where the focus was on spiritual music. In 1943, it housed the Grand Ole Opry, the epicenter of country music, where they say Bill Monroe invented bluegrass music. In between, it was a theater where Harry Houdini, Charlie Chaplin, Helen Keller, and other celebrities filled its 2,632 seats. After a long timeout and some major upgrades, it's once again used as one of Nashville's most impressive concert venues.

The modern **Schermerhorn Symphony Center** is the place to go for classical music with the Nashville Symphony.

Unlike *other* Halls of Fame in the area, the **Musicians Hall of Fame** gives props to musicians of *all* musical genres, going all the way back to the first wax recordings. Exhibits include famous instruments, costumes, and many plaques. It's currently located in the historic Nashville Municipal Auditorium.

You can see all kinds of big-name shows and concerts at the 20,000 seat **Bridgestone Arena**. Ideally, the Nashville Predators hockey team won't be playing a home game at the same time.

Nashville

Festivals!

Sure, Nashville has a world-class reputation for its concert halls, its Halls of Fame, its Oprys, and its honky tonks. But there are still *more* ways to soak up Nashville's culture scene. All through the year, the area hosts festivals that celebrate the best of Nashville: the music, the arts, the crafts, the music, the food, the drinks, the kids, the music, the games, the theater, the music, and the music. Come take a look!

Tomato Art Fest: "Uniting fruits and vegetables since 2004," this fun-filled festival is hard to describe. There's music, of course. Plus all kinds of art, food, wacky contests, kids' events, and it's totally free. Everyone is encouraged to wear a costume.

Nashville Cultural Festival: This is everyone's festival, sharing traditions and celebrating more than 50 cultures found in Nashville's diverse population. There is food, dance, music, visual arts, and a very popular children's area.

Music City Hot Chicken Festival: This festival celebrates the crispy, spicy Nashville favorite. It starts, fittingly, with a fire truck parade. It ends with plunging your burning mouth into a firehose. In between, there's an amateur cooking competition, music, and plenty of milder food for those who enjoy protecting their taste buds!

CMA Music Fest: The official four-day festival of the people who bring you the Country Music Awards! Guess what kind of music is played?

Fiddlers Jamboree: Bluegrass music was born around Nashville, and the annual Fiddlers Jamboree along the Harpeth River brings together many of the world's best fiddlers and other musicians.

Nashville 49

How to Talk
Nashville

Just about every place in the world has some words that only make sense to locals. Here are a few examples of "only in Nashville" words or phrases.

Stompin' grounds

Where you or your people are from.

ATHENS OF THE SOUTH

Maybe because of the city's 30-plus colleges. Maybe for the Parthenon. Maybe both.

MEAT & THREE

Dinner down South, with meat and three side dishes. One is definitely mashed potatoes and gravy. One of the others might be Jell-o or mac and cheese.

Vols

The University of Tennessee sports teams. Short for the "Volunteers."

Fixin'

It's like sayin' you're plannin' to do somethin'.

Honky-Tonk

A lively, bouncy style of country and western music (and also describing places where you can here this music played)

Swarmageddon

What happens when those disgusting cicadas arrive all summer.

NASHVILLE: It's Weird!

If you think a Greek Parthenon in Tennessee is weird, that's just the tip of the mountain.

Jurassic Lawn: What's weirder than a life-size (but not living) lion, tiger, and bear guarding a Bellevue lawn? How about the life-size dinosaur statues like this one roaming the property? From the road you can see a realistic T. rex, stegosaur, ultrasaur, ankylodon, velociraptors . . . and watch for more! This private property (keep off the grass!) belongs to George Boedecker, who founded the Crocs shoe company. What, no crocodiles?

Who Goes There: Friend or Foam? If you see a swordfight in Elmington Park, and the fighters are dressed in medieval garb, and it's Sunday, good news . . . the weapons are made of foam! The combat group Dur Demarion (a Lord of the Rings reference) takes their play seriously. Newcomers are welcome—they'll lend you gear. Fight safely!

Best. Bathrooms. Ever. There's even a Hall of Fame for America's Best Bathroom. Seriously! Nashville has two winners: the elegant, green-tiled throne rooms in Nashville's art deco Hermitage Hotel (above) and the Nashville Zoo "loo." If you don't believe it, you can see the official plaques yourself. They're flush against the walls.

FAST FACT

Cotton candy was invented in 1908 by Nashville dentist William Morrison and candymaker John Wharton. Now, *that's* a sweet, sweet way to grow a business!

What People Do
IN NASHVILLE

Nashville is more than tunes and tourism. Big business is humming in the Music City.

Education:

With more than 27,000 employees, Vanderbilt University (and medical center) is the area's largest employer. Add 12,000+ students and you've got enough people to fill a small city!

Music:

It will not surprise you by now that more than 50,000 people in Nashville make their living in the music business in one way or the other!

vroom!

Nissan, one of the world's largest car and truck manufacturers has its US headquarters in nearby Franklin, Tennessee.

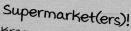

Supermarket(ers)!

Kroger, a major grocery store chain, is also a major Nashville employer.

Healthcare:

A healthy percentage of the Nashville area's workers work in medical centers, hospitals, and with health providers.

Taylor Swift

In 2003, at 14, Taylor was laser-focused on a career in country music. So she convinced her parents to move from Reading, Pennsylvania, to the Nashville area. By 16, her first album, *Taylor Swift*, became a top-200 country album—for 157 weeks! She's lived in Nashville ever since.

Billy Ray and Miley Cyrus
Like father, like daughter? Guess which Cyrus has
been a legend in pop, rock, and country music, as well
as a Disney TV star? Both of them! Billy Ray and his
daughter Miley are both big Nashville celebrities.

The Country Music Hall of Fame and Museum

This place is the centerpiece of Music City. The museum and entertainment complex wears many (cowboy) hats. It honors the past, and looks toward the future of country music.

CMA Theater: What's a music museum without a place for live music? With 776 seats, the CMA theater is a world-class venue to see (and hear) a show.

The Country Music Hall of Fame! Getting accepted in the Hall of Fame is the biggest honor country music artists and professionals can get. They're chosen each year by fellow singers, musicians, songwriters, executives, and broadcasters. Then, each year, they throw the winners—and themselves—a big concert party.

The Country Music Museum: This huge interactive museum is the largest of its kind. In gallery after gallery, visitors explore famous instruments, stage costumes, a recording studio, cool celebrity cars, and much more. Visitors can listen to over a million audio and video recordings spanning country music's rich history.

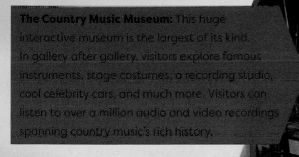

FAST FACT

Notice something familiar about the Hall of Fame's windows? That's right, they look like piano keys!

Hatch Show Print: It's a restored, old-style print shop that's been producing concert posters, and much more, for more than 140 years. Tour the original printing machines, see thousands of historic concert posters, and even make your own print masterpieces!

Nashville 59

Eat the Nashville Way

In Nashville, the local food is also a delicious American history lesson. You might arrive hungry, but you won't leave that way!

Hot Chicken: Fried chicken is a Southern tradition, and Nashville's particular poultry pride and joy. Hot chicken is crispy, juicy, and fried, with hot sauce, black pepper, cayenne pepper, and chili powder added. It originated at the beloved Hattie B's restaurant. Be sure to get plenty to drink to cool off your mouth!

NASHVILLE'S
GooGoo
SINCE 1912

Local Candy: Nashville's sweet treat is a chocolate-and-nuts candy called Goo-Goo Clusters, made here since 1912.

Fried Pickles: The name pretty much says it all. They're pickles, and they're fried like chicken. A local favorite.

Meat and Three: Whatever meat you want, when you order it with three side dishes, you're getting a "meat and three." Favorite sides include mashed potatoes and gravy, coleslaw, spicy beans, mac and cheese, fried okra, and cornbread. Don't forget your sweet tea!

Banana Pudding: Is it a dessert? Or is it a side dish? Once you taste it, you'll want it for both! Nashville's sweet, rich banana pudding is usually topped with vanilla wafer cookies and some whipped cream.

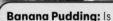

Barbecue: The word "barbecue" means different things in different places. In Nashville, the sauce is thick and tangy, while the meats are smoky and juicy. Some locals like coleslaw dropped on top.

Go, Nashville Sports!

Tennessee takes its sports teams VERY seriously! The fans in Nashville share their team love with Memphis, and the rest of the state. Here's who they're rooting for:

Derrick Henry

TENNESSEE TITANS

Joined the American Football League as the Houston Oilers in 1960. Joined the NFL in 1970. Moved and became the Tennessee Oilers in 1997, then became Nashville's Tennessee Titans in 1999.

Won the American Football Conference (AFC) championship in 1999, but lost the Super Bowl to the St. Louis Rams.

Cool Stuff: Only NFL team to field two runners with 2000-plus yards in a season: Chris Johnson in 2009 and Derrick Henry in 2020.

Big Names: Steve McNair, Warren Moon, Bruce Matthews, Eddie George, Derrick Henry, Chris Johnson.

Home: Nissan Stadium

Ja Morant

MEMPHIS GRIZZLIES

Joined the National Basketball Association (NBA) in 1995 as the Vancouver Grizzlies. Became the Memphis Grizzlies in 2001, as part of the NBA's Western Conference. And yes, we know it's not in Nashville! But it's close!

Won The Grizz have made it to the playoffs 12 times in twenty years since moving to Memphis.

Cool Stuff: There was an earlier NBA team called the Memphis Grizzlies, which played for a year in 1974!

Big Names: Zach Randolph, Pau Gasol, Marc Gasol, Mike Conley Jr., Ja Morant, Jonas Valančiūnas

Home: FedExForum

If you look on a map, you'll see that Memphis is pretty far east for a Western Conference team!

NASHVILLE PREDATORS

Joined the National Hockey League (NHL) in 1998.

Won Played in the 2017 Stanley Cup Final.

Cool Stuff: The Nashville fans voted for their team name from these choices: the Attack, the Fury, the Ice Tigers, and the Predators. The Preds have a sabretooth tiger for their mascot.

Big Names: David Legwand, Shea Weber, Roman Josi, Martin Erat, Pekka Rinne, Craig Smith

Home: Bridgestone Arena

NASHVILLE SC SOCCER CLUB

Joined the National Premier Soccer League (NPSL) in 2017; moved to Major League Soccer (MLS) in 2020.

The mascot for the team is a coyote. The fans haven't settled on a nickname for themselves yet. Thoughts?

Cool Stuff: The team's owners include Tennessee Titans' power rusher Derrick Henry and the actress Reese Witherspoon. The Nashville SC logo is a big N with sound waves, to represent the music city.

Big Names: Hany Mukhtar, C.J. Sapong, David Romney, Alex Muyl, Walker Zimmerman, Randall Leal

Home: GEODIS Park

Randall Leal

Take It Outside!

Nashville is an outdoor lover's paradise. You can walk, run, bike, golf, kayak, and do lots more.

There are two ways to stay cool in the hot Nashville summers: shady trees and breeze. Combine them both and you're ziplining through the **Fontanel Zipline Forest**! There are eight ziplines, reaching as high as 85 feet in the air!

The tallest waterfall east of the Rocky Mountains isn't Niagara Falls. It's the 256-foot-high **Fall Creek Falls**. Experience about five miles of hiking, cross a gorge on suspended bridges, and see four other high waterfalls, all in the same day!

Ready for a great scenic run or walk? There are nearly **80 miles of greenway trails** in the city, from downtown to the shores of the Cumberland River, spreading out in different directions. You'll cover trails, parks, and even Centennial Park itself.

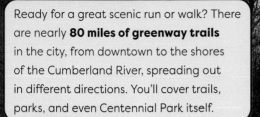

Percy Priest isn't a person. It's the name of Nashville area's largest lake. It's got more than 250 miles of shoreline, which is plenty of space for boating, fishing, and even camping. If you don't want to catch and cook your own dinner, there are floating restaurants, or you can stretch out and picnic on the beach.

Want a deeper appreciation of the region? Go spelunking in some of the longest caves anywhere. The **Cumberland Caverns** span nearly 30 miles. You can explore great crystal formations, and the 600 foot long, 140 foot high "Hall of the Mountain King." And hold your breath if you want to get through the 11-inch-wide "Lemon Squeezer" passage!

COLLEGE TOWN

Nashville is home to many top colleges, including leading Historically Black Universities.

VANDERBILT UNIVERSITY

Founded 1873
Students: 13,500+
Popular majors: Economics, social sciences, computer science, math, neuroscience
Fast Fact: Railroad and shipping tycoon Cornelius Vanderbilt donated the school's first $1,000,000. Now the school has an $11 billion endowment.

TENNESSEE STATE UNIVERSITY

Founded 1912
Students: 8,000
Popular majors: Business, criminal justice/law enforcement, communication, health professions, teacher education
Fast Fact: TSU is Tennessee's only public Historically Black University.

BELMONT UNIVERSITY

Founded 1890
Students: 6,600
Popular majors: Music business, audio engineering, commercial music, songwriting, nursing
Fast Fact: Belmont began as a women's college, and now produces a lot of music producers.

FISK UNIVERSITY

Founded 1866
Students: 900
Popular majors: biology, business, psychology, political science, English language and literature
Fast Fact: Fisk's elegant campus is a historical landmark. The Fisk Jubilee Singers are world famous.

AMERICAN BAPTIST COLLEGE

Founded 1924
Students: 150
Popular majors: Theology, human services, entrepreneurship studies
Fast Fact: Though mainly training Baptist ministers, ABC has produced many prominent civil rights leaders.

Vanderbilt University

LOL!
Laugh with Nashville

If 8 is A and 9 is B, which US State comes next?

10 is C (Tennessee)

What did one Nashville pickle say to the other just before the weekend?

Oh, no! It's Fry-Day!

What's the difference between an opera and the Opry?

You're supposed to sit quietly at the opera!

Where are you if you're surrounded by sabretooth tigers?

At a Nashville Predators hockey game!

What do you call crickets, bullfrogs, and owls making noise in the Nashville woods?

Country music!

What do you call a group of sweet babies in Nashville?

A Goo-Goo Cluster!

Why is a good Nashville banjo player like a happy person with boogers?

Because they're both "pickin' and grinnin'"!

Why did the hot chicken cross the road?

To get a drink of cold water!

GO TO THE Park

The Nashville area has 178 parks and 99 miles of greenway that cover more than 15,000 acres. No wonder there's so much going on outdoors!

Centennial Park

Not far from downtown, Centennial Park offers more than its famous 1897 Parthenon. The 132-acre park features athletic facilities, an arts activity center, a sunken garden, and Cockrill Springs, a natural spring.

Percy and Edwin Warner were brothers and Nashville park commissioners. The parkland was donated by Percy's daughter, Percie. Really.

EDWIN WARNER PARK
606.7 acres

Edwin Warner (1870-1945) succeeded his brother Percy on the Park Board in 1927 and served for eighteen years. He personally directed the acquisition of most of the Warner Park acreage and supervised WPA development of the property. Warner organized a major Victory Garden program in the park during WWII. Park land west of Old Hickory Blvd. was renamed in his honor in 1937.

THE HISTORICAL COMMISSION OF METROPOLITAN NASHVILLE AND DAVIDSON COUNTY
NO. 50   ERECTED 1985

The Warner Parks

The biggest parks (by far) are the side-by-side Warner Parks: Edwin Warner Park and Percy Warner Park. Together, at more than 3,000 acres, they're one of America's largest urban parks. Park buildings are also historic landmarks.

In addition to two golf courses, miles of trails (for humans and horses), and athletic fields, there's a horse racing track, the Iroquois Steeplechase. Each year they hold the Harpeth Hills Flying Monkey Marathon. Really.

It's Alive! Animals in Nashville

Sure, there's lots of nightlife in Nashville. But did you know about all the wildlife?

Salamanders Galore: Ever wonder where the salamander capital of the world is? Wonder no more! There are more than 30 species of salamander in nearby Great Smoky Mountains National Park! But don't touch them—salamander skin is poisonous. Though it won't kill you, your skin and eyes will burn. And you thought the *chicken* was hot in Nashville!

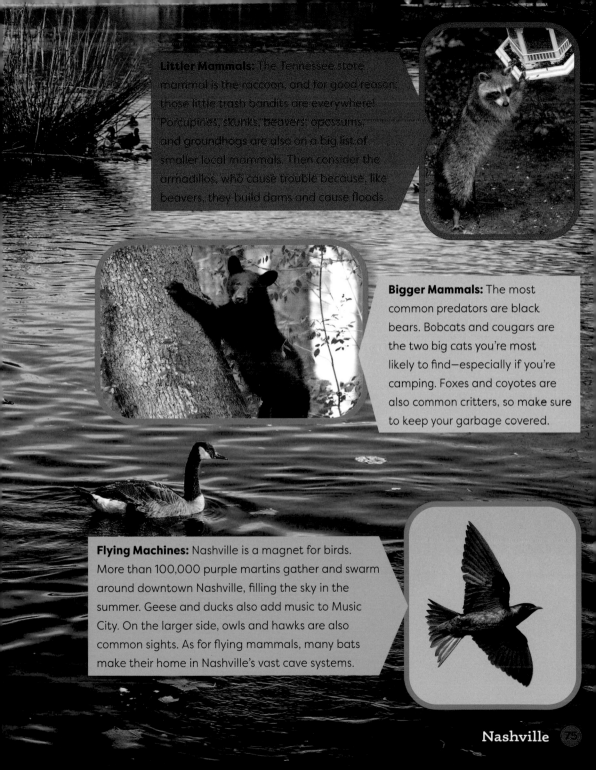

Littler Mammals: The Tennessee state mammal is the raccoon, and for good reason: those little trash bandits are everywhere! Porcupines, skunks, beavers, opossums, and groundhogs are also on a big list of smaller local mammals. Then consider the armadillos, who cause trouble because, like beavers, they build dams and cause floods.

Bigger Mammals: The most common predators are black bears. Bobcats and cougars are the two big cats you're most likely to find—especially if you're camping. Foxes and coyotes are also common critters, so make sure to keep your garbage covered.

Flying Machines: Nashville is a magnet for birds. More than 100,000 purple martins gather and swarm around downtown Nashville, filling the sky in the summer. Geese and ducks also add music to Music City. On the larger side, owls and hawks are also common sights. As for flying mammals, many bats make their home in Nashville's vast cave systems.

WE SAW IT AT THE ZOO

The Nashville Zoo at Grassmere is one of the country's newer zoos, having opened in 1990 at the historic Dunn Farm, an early slaveholding plantation. Inside the zoo, you'll find more than 6,200 animals from nearly 350 species. There are modern habitats for many common zoo animals, as well as the uncommon galloways, bonteboks, devons, and tamarins.

FAST FACT

The 188-acre zoo has a strong focus on animal conservation and preserving endangered species, such as cheetahs and clouded leopards.

Andean bear

Sumatran tiger

Southern White Rhinoceros

Lorikeet

FAST FACT

The Kids love the **Jungle Gym**, a huge (66,000 sq.ft.) Jungle-themed playground built by thousands of local volunteers.

NASHVILLE BY THE NUMBERS

Stats and facts and digits . . . galore! Here are some of the numbers that make Nashvile what it is.

365

Days of the year when live music can be found in Nashville. Of course, that's 366 during leap years!

20,000

Number of chewy, chocolate Goo-Goo Clusters that the Standard Candy Company can make in an hour.

1

Is your family moving? Nashville was ranked No. 1 in the US for people buying their first home!

93

Stars (and counting) along the Music City Walk of Fame, honoring those who've added to Nashville's musical heritage.

60,000

People employed by the music industry, the most in any city on earth.

200+

Number of songs Elvis Presley recorded at Nashville's historic RCA Studio B.

95.5

Radio dial location of Nashville's WSM-FM, the first FM radio station in the United States.

Spooky Sights

Do you believe in ghosts and spirits? Not everyone does . . . but no one knows for sure! Like most cities, Nashville has lots of places that people say are haunted.

When it opened in 1898, **Tennessee State Prison** was a big, creepy building. When it was closed in 1992, it was called dangerous and overcrowded. Plus it was a hundred years old. They say some of the 125 prisoners executed there over the years can still be heard clanging metal, or even screaming as they wander the eerie stone halls.

Did farmer John Bell swindle his neighbor Kate Batts in 1817? She thought so, and she swore to haunt his land forever. The house is gone, but people who've visited the **Bell Witch Cave** hear groans, some feel their hair getting pulled, and others feel like they're being pinched!

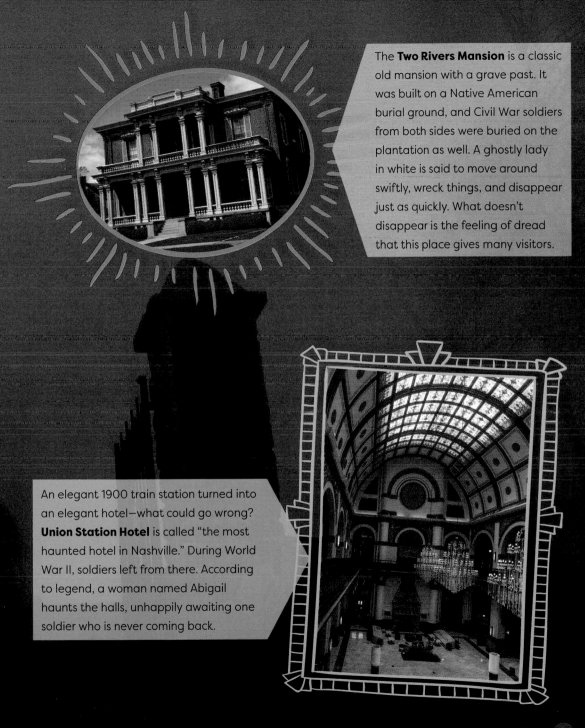

The **Two Rivers Mansion** is a classic old mansion with a grave past. It was built on a Native American burial ground, and Civil War soldiers from both sides were buried on the plantation as well. A ghostly lady in white is said to move around swiftly, wreck things, and disappear just as quickly. What doesn't disappear is the feeling of dread that this place gives many visitors.

An elegant 1900 train station turned into an elegant hotel—what could go wrong? **Union Station Hotel** is called "the most haunted hotel in Nashville." During World War II, soldiers left from there. According to legend, a woman named Abigail haunts the halls, unhappily awaiting one soldier who is never coming back.

On BROADWAY

Most visitors who come to Nashville are attracted to the bright neon lights of Broadway. Not the street in New York City, but the long avenue that runs through downtown Music City. Like New York's, it's packed with entertainment, shopping, and tons of endless people-watching!

Broadway has history! There are many grand, historic buildings lining Broadway. The Old Post Office is now the Frist Center for the Visual Arts, while the old Union Train Station is now a haunted hotel. And that amazing gothic castle? That's the Hume-Fogg High School. Check out the carved stone figures, and "figure" out which ones represent math, science, art, or literature.

The Honky-Tonk Highway: Music lovers from around the world trek up and down Broadway to hear live music. On any night, legions of visitors amble between honky-tonk saloons, outdoor locales, and even larger concert venues on Broadway. From the street, you might hear several bands at once!

ERNEST TUBB
RECORD SHOP

REAL COUNTRY MUSIC
LIVES HERE
OUR 74TH YEAR

Tubbs of Music: Of Broadway's many bright signs, perhaps the most famous is the giant guitar hovering over Ernest Tubb's Record Shop, a landmark for finding new and old music, books, and other Nashville memorabilia since 1947.

Boot Up : Well-heeled country music lovers love cowboy boots. And Broadway's got more boot stores than just about anywhere! The boots you'll find are more than just footwear—they're unique leather and metal works of art.

Every year!

Here are the annual events that happen in Nashville just about every year. What do you want to do?

The **Iroquois Steeplechase** is a horse race (named for a horse, not for the Iroquois people), held each May since 1941. The race lasts a few minutes, but the party lasts over a long weekend for about 25,000 visitors.

Every September, the three-day **African Street Festival** brings traditions, food, music, dance, costumes, and crafts from across the Atlantic Ocean.

Wilson County Fair
Featuring games, rides, food, and all the farm animals you can count, all to show off what's happening in the Nashville area.

June 19 is the day to celebrate the **Juneteenth Block Party**, a big musical event celebrating the emancipation of America's enslaved people in 1865.

Nashville 85

Not Far Away

Mammoth Cave National Park (KY) is the longest system of caves in the world. Its 400-mile network of well-marked passages is a UNESCO heritage site, meaning it's supported by the United Nations. Famous features include the Rainbow Dome, Crystal Lake, and the Snowball Room. It's an easy 90 minutes from Nashville, and the experience is worth every minute of travel.

Do you know what spelunking is?

Um, does that mean flunking a spelling test?

Ha! No, it means cave exploring!

Oh! Caves . . . man!

We went about 90 minutes from Nashville to see **Mammoth Cave National Park**.

It's the largest cave system in the world!

Yikes! I hope you didn't do all of them

No, but what we saw was amazing. There are huge underground domes, a lake, and weird rock formations.

Sounds like an underground wonderland.

Yup! And here's what it looks like when the park ranger turns off the lights.

Ha-ha, very funny!

We went for an underground boat ride at a different cave.

Wait . . . what? How? Explain, please.

The **Craighead Caverns** are in Sweetwater, Tennessee. There's a huge underground lake called the Lost Sea.

Well, I guess it's not lost anymore.

Ha! It's the largest one of those anywhere! And you can take a boat ride!

Look, ma, no paddles!

The boat has a glass bottom, so we peered down on underwater rock formations!

Okay, that's just spooky!

The lake was discovered by a kid who had to squeeze through a thin tunnel.

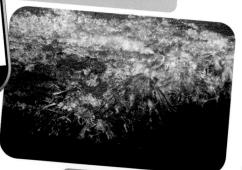

Uh, glad that was not me! 😵!

Chill! The tunnel is bigger now! If you're too scared, there are great nature hikes on the land over the cave, too.

Wow, arts and crafts class was never like this!

What do you mean?

We just left the **Appalachian Center for Craft**—it was amazing!

Where is it?

To the east of Nashville, at Tennessee Tech. If you can make it with your hands, artists make it here!

Glass, jewelry, pottery, weaving, sculpture, and lots more!

Sounds pretty busy!

And they even have workshops and classes for us to learn!

Here's a good one: How can a river be called lazy if it's always moving?

Hm. I don't know. How?

When it's moving reeeeaallly slooooowly!

That's like my slowpoke brother!

We went on a lazy river float in **Kingston Springs**.

Oh, that looks very pleasant!

It was! We just floated along, looking at the trees and the sky and the other floaters!

One trick though: You need one float and two cars.

Huh?

Well, you have to leave a car at the end of the float . . . then drive back to the start. You float down, pile into the second car, then drive back to the start.

Sounds confusing.

Well, it's easier than floating back UP the river!

Good point!

Sister Cities Around the World

In the 1950s, not long after World War II, people looked for new ways to create connections between nations. The Sister Cities program was born. These cities team up in different ways, not only exchanging cultures, but business and education opportunities as well.

Nashville's Sister Cities

- Edmonton, Canada
- Belfast, Northern Ireland
- Caen, France
- Magdeburg, Germany
- Taiyuan, China
- Kamakura, Japan
- Chengdu, China
- Tamworth, Australia
- Mendoza, Argentina

Sister Cities in Action
Here are some ways Nashville is working with its sister cities.

Caen, France: Nashville's first sister city, their connections run from the cooperative (academic exchanges) to the competitive (inter-city basketball games).

Kamakura, Japan: This city is known for temples and shrines as well as beaches and entertainment. Collaborations and exchanges between these two cities have extended beyond the arts and leisure to include business ventures from both nations.

Edmonton, Canada: This 1,000,000+ capital city of the Canadian province of Alberta is often called "festival city." Arts and culture events are hosted here, and exchanges with Nashville happen often.

Mendoza, Argentina: Time definitely slows down in Mendoza, in South America's Andes Mountains. Oil and wine are crushed and bottled. Horses and rafts are ridden. Mendoza's Rivers and mountains are appreciated and explored daily by locals and travelers alike. Sound familiar?

FIND OUT MORE!

Books, Websites, and More!

Books

Bertholf, Bret. *The Long Gone Lonesome History of Country Music.* Little Brown Books for Young Readers, 2007.

Erlic, Lily. *Nashville (American Cities).* Weigl, 2020.

Harris, Beatrice. *The Trail of Tears (A Look at U.S. History).* Gareth Stevens, 2021.

Hewson, Anthony. *Nashville SC (Inside MLS).* Sportszone, 2021.

Tieck, Sarah. *Tennessee: Explore the United States.* Big Buddy Books, 2019.

Wallace, Sandra Neil. *Love Is Loud: How Diane Nash Led the Civil Rights Movement.* Simon & Schuster/Wiseman, 2023.

Web Sites

www.VisitMusicCity.com

The official tourism website of Nashville's Convention & Visitors Corp.

www.Timeout.com/Nashville

A current list of things to do and things happening in Nashville now! Includes kids activities.

https://tennesseehistory.org

Learn lots more about the city and the state with the Tennessee Historical Society.

www.Nashville.gov

Nashville's official city website, including local news and events.

Photo Credits and Thanks

Photos from Dreamstime, Shutterstock, or Wikimedia except:
AP Photo: The Tennessean 21TR; Mark Humphrey 22B; Susan Walsh 24T. Courtesy of Dur Demarion: 53R. Newscom: Randy Litzinger 65B; Clarence Holmes/Agefotostock 84; Steve Roberts/Cal Sports Media 85B.

Artwork: LemonadePixel; Maps (6-7): Jessica Nevins.

Thanks to our pals Nancy Ellwood, Kait Leggett, and the fine folks at Arcadia!

INDEX

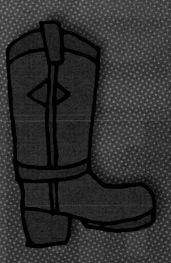

Thanks for Visiting

NASHVILLE

Come Back Soon!